C000247011

## by Iain Gray

# Lang**Syne**
### PUBLISHING
WRITING *to* REMEMBER

LangSyne
**PUBLISHING**
WRITING *to* REMEMBER

79 Main Street, Newtongrange,
Midlothian EH22 4NA
Tel: 0131 344 0414
E-mail: info@lang-syne.co.uk
www.langsyneshop.co.uk

Design by Dorothy Meikle
Printed by Printwell Ltd
© Lang Syne Publishers Ltd 2022

ISBN 978-1-85217-466-8

# Hall

**MOTTO:**
Live so that you may live.

**CREST:**
The head of the hunting hound
known as a Talbot.

**TERRITORY:**
The Borders and Renfrewshire.

**NAME** variations include:
Ha
Hal
Hale
Halle
Haugh
Haule

*Echoes of a far distant past
can still be found in most names*

*Chapter one:*

# Origins of
# Scottish surnames

by George Forbes

**It all began with the Normans.**

For it was they who introduced surnames into common usage more than a thousand years ago, initially based on the title of their estates, local villages and chateaux in France to distinguish and identify these landholdings, usually acquired at the point of a bloodstained sword.

Such grand descriptions also helped enhance the prestige of these arrogant warlords and generally glorify their lofty positions high above the humble serfs slaving away below in the pecking order who only had single names, often with Biblical connotations as in Pierre and Jacques.

The only descriptive distinctions among this peasantry concerned their occupations, like Pierre the swineherd or Jacques the ferryman.

The Normans themselves were originally Vikings (or Northmen) who raided, colonised and eventually settled down around the French coastline.

They had sailed up the Seine in their longboats in 900 AD under their ferocious leader Rollo and ruled the roost in north east France before sailing over to conquer England, bringing their relatively new tradition of having surnames with them.

It took another hundred years for the Normans to percolate northwards and surnames did not begin to appear in Scotland until the thirteenth century.

These adventurous knights brought an aura of chivalry with them and it was said no damsel of any distinction would marry a man unless he had at least two names.

The family names included that of Scotland's great hero Robert De Brus and his compatriots were warriors from families like the De Morevils, De Umphravils, De Berkelais, De Quincis, De Viponts and De Vaux.

As the knights settled the boundaries of their vast estates, they took territorial names, as in Hamilton, Moray, Crawford, Cunningham, Dunbar, Ross, Wemyss, Dundas, Galloway, Renfrew, Greenhill, Hazelwood, Sandylands and Church-hill.

Other names, though not with any obvious geographical or topographical features, nevertheless derived from ancient parishes like Douglas, Forbes, Dalyell and Guthrie.

Other surnames were coined in connection with occupations, castles or legendary deeds. Stuart originated in the word steward, a prestigious post which was an integral part of any large medieval household. The same applied to Cooks, Chamberlains, Constables and Porters.

Borders towns and forts – needed in areas like the Debateable Lands which were constantly fought over by feuding local families – had their own distinctive names; and it was often from them that the resident groups took their communal titles, as in the Grahams of Annandale, the Elliots and Armstrongs of the East Marches, the Scotts and Kerrs of Teviotdale and Eskdale.

Even physical attributes crept into surnames, as in Small, Little and More (the latter being 'beg' in Gaelic), Long or Lang, Stark, Stout, Strong or Strang and even Jolly.

Mieklejohns would have had the strength of several men, while Littlejohn was named after the legendary sidekick of Robin Hood.

Colours got into the act with Black, White, Grey, Brown and Green (Red developed into Reid,

Ruddy or Ruddiman). Blue was rare and nobody ever wanted to be associated with yellow.

Pompous worthies took the name Wiseman, Goodman and Goodall.

Words intimating the sons of leading figures were soon affiliated into the language as in Johnson, Adamson, Richardson and Thomson, while the Norman equivalent of Fitz (from the French-Latin 'filius' meaning 'son') cropped up in Fitzmaurice and Fitzgerald.

The prefix 'Mac' was 'son of' in Gaelic and clans often originated with occupations – as in MacNab being sons of the Abbot, MacPherson and MacVicar being sons of the minister and MacIntosh being sons of the chief.

The church's influence could be found in the names Kirk, Clerk, Clarke, Bishop, Friar and Monk. Proctor came from a church official, Singer and Sangster from choristers, Gilchrist and Gillies from Christ's servant, Mitchell, Gilmory and Gilmour from servants of St Michael and Mary, Malcolm from a servant of Columba and Gillespie from a bishop's servant.

The rudimentary medical profession was represented by Barber (a trade which also once included dentistry and surgery) as well as Leech or Leitch.

Businessmen produced Merchants, Mercers, Monypennies, Chapmans, Sellers and Scales, while down at the old village watermill the names that cropped up included Miller, Walker and Fuller.

Other self explanatory trades included Coopers, Brands, Barkers, Tanners, Skinners, Brewsters and Brewers, Tailors, Saddlers, Wrights, Cartwrights, Smiths, Harpers, Joiners, Sawyers, Masons and Plumbers.

Even the scenery was utilised as in Craig, Moor, Hill, Glen, Wood and Forrest.

Rank, whether high or low, took its place with Laird, Barron, Knight, Tennant, Farmer, Husband, Granger, Grieve, Shepherd, Shearer and Fletcher.

The hunt and the chase supplied Hunter, Falconer, Fowler, Fox, Forrester, Archer and Spearman.

The renowned medieval historian Froissart, who eulogised about the romantic deeds of chivalry (and who condemned Scotland as being a poverty stricken wasteland), once sniffily dismissed the peasantry of his native France as the jacquerie (or the jacques-without-names) but it was these same humble folk who ended up overthrowing the arrogant aristocracy.

In the olden days, only the blueblooded knights of antiquity were entitled to full, proper names, both Christian and surnames, but with the passing of time and a more egalitarian, less feudal atmosphere, more respectful and worthy titles spread throughout the populace as a whole.

Echoes of a far distant past can still be found in most names and they can be borne with pride in commemoration of past generations who fought and toiled in some capacity or other to make our nation what it now is, for good or ill.

Meanwhile, many families proudly boast the heraldic device known as a Coat of Arms, as featured on our front cover.

The central motif of the Coat of Arms would originally have been what was sometimes borne on the shield of a warrior to distinguish himself from others on the battlefield.

Not featured on the Coat of Arms, but high-lighted on page three, is the family motto and related crest – with the latter frequently different from the central motif.

*Chapter two:*

# Murder and mayhem

**A name derived from the Norman French de Aula, Hall is both a locational and an occupational surname denoting someone who lived, or worked, in a hall.**

In medieval times, the 'hall' in question would have been a manorial hall, or home of anyone wealthy enough to employ live-in servants, such as a steward to handle domestic and business accounts.

The name is first recorded in Lincolnshire, England, where a family of Fitz Williams had settled in the wake of the Norman invasion of 1066.

Greatford Hall became their family seat, and it was in order to differentiate himself from his older brother that Arthur Fitz William changed his surname to Hall – as in Greatford Hall – in about 1090.

While the Fitz Williams and Halls continued to flourish in Lincolnshire, a branch of the Halls were among the many Anglo-Norman families who eventually settled in Scotland.

Some of these nobles had found refuge in Scotland under King Malcolm Canmore following an abortive rebellion against William of Normandy in 1070, while there was a further influx at the invitation of David I during his reign from 1124 to 1153.

The Halls who settled in Scotland split into two separate branches.

One was granted the lands of Glenryg, Berwickshire, in the Borders, while the other became established as the de Aulas, or Halls, of Fulbar, Renfrewshire.

One noted member of the Renfrewshire branch was Thomas Hall, whose faithful service as personal physician to Scotland's Robert II, who reigned from 1371 to 1390, was rewarded with the grant of the lands of Staneley, in Renfrewshire.

By about 1550, however, the direct line of the Renfrewshire Halls had died out.

It was in the Borders territory that the Halls were destined to stamp their own particular mark on the pages of Scotland's turbulent history as infamous reivers.

These reivers took their name from their lawless custom of reiving, or raiding, not only their neighbours' livestock, but also that of their neighbours across the border.

The word 'bereaved', for example, indicating

to have suffered loss, derives from the original 'reived', meaning to have suffered loss of property.

A Privy Council report of 1608 graphically described how the 'wild incests, adulteries, convocation of the lieges, shooting and wearing of hackbuts, pistols, lances, daily bloodshed, oppression, and disobedience in civil matters, neither are nor has been punished.'

A constant thorn in the flesh of both the English and Scottish authorities was the cross-border raiding and pillaging carried out by well-mounted and heavily armed men, the contingent from the Scottish side of the border known and feared as 'moss troopers.'

In an attempt to bring order to what was known as the wild 'debateable land' on both sides of the border, Alexander II of Scotland had in 1237 signed the Treaty of York, which for the first time established the Scottish border with England as a line running from the Solway to the Tweed.

On either side of the border there were three 'marches' or areas of administration, the West, East and Middle Marches, and a warden governed these.

Complaints from either side of the border were dealt with on Truce Days, when the wardens of the different marches would act as arbitrators.

There was also a law known as the Hot Trod, that granted anyone who had their livestock stolen the right to pursue the thieves and recover their property.

In the Scottish borderlands, the Homes, Halls and Swintons dominated the East March, while the Armstrongs, Maxwells, Johnstones and Grahams were the rulers of the West March.

The Kerrs, along with the Douglases and Elliots, held sway in the Middle March.

The Halls were to be found on both sides of the border – at Redesdale in England and, as noted, in the Scottish East March – particularly in Liddesdale and East Teviotdale.

One source has described these Halls as having been considered a clan to whom no quarter should be given, adding they were feared and hated in equal measure on both sides of the border.

Infamous bearers of the name included Eddie Hall, described in contemporary accounts as 'a notorious thief', and George Hall of Borduff described in 1597 as 'a notorious thief and murderer.'

It was following the Union of the Crowns in 1603 that James I (James VI of Scotland) attempted to crush the Border mayhem once and for all.

The very term 'Borders' was abolished and

renamed 'the Middle Shires', while scores of particularly unruly families were forcibly uprooted and either conscripted into military service or banished to Ireland.

In later centuries, it was many of these Scots-Irish Halls who found new lives for themselves in North America, Australia and New Zealand and where their descendants can be found today.

Exile to Ireland, meanwhile, did not always deter the Halls – given a suitable opportunity they simply made their way back to their native Borders.

One such character was John Hall of Elsdon, more colourfully known as Long Parcies Jocke.

A contemporary account laments how he had 'returned out of Ireland, by what pass we know not, a riotous liver, ill-reputed and much suspected, having nothing to maintain himself with but by keeping an alehouse.'

When not embroiled in internecine Border feuds, the Halls found themselves at the centre of the religious and political upheavals of the tumultuous seventeenth century.

Born in Kirkcudbright, in the southwest of Scotland, in 1559, John Hall was the Moderator of the General Assembly of the Church of Scotland who, in

1616, co-authored the controversial *Confession of Faith and Catechism*.

Minister at Leith, near Edinburgh, at the time, the catechism was in direct opposition to the religious observance demanded by James I as set out in his equally controversial *Articles of Perth* – and Hall was summarily 'banished' by the Privy Council to Montrose, where he died in 1627.

Eleven years after his death, a National Covenant, pledging defence of the Presbyterian religion, was signed in the Greyfriars Kirk, Edinburgh.

Copies were circulated throughout Scotland, and the hundreds of ordinary men and women who subscribed to it, then and later, became known as Covenanters – and among them was the prominent Covenanting leader Henry Hall, laird of Haughhead, in the Borders area of Teviotdale.

Following the restoration to the throne of Charles II in 1660, the death knell for the Covenanting movement was sounded when a Recissory Act was passed, declaring the Covenant illegal.

Episcopal rule was foisted on the Scottish Church, and all ministers who refused to adhere to this new order were deprived of their parishes.

Along with their congregations, many

ministers literally took to the hills, preaching at open-air meetings known as conventicles.

Lookouts were posted to keep a wary eye out for the approach of Government troops, known as dragoons, and justice was executed on the spot for those unfortunate enough to fall into their hands.

Constantly persecuted by the forces of authority, the Covenanters rose in futile rebellion in November of 1666 and, as a sign of the harsh treatment that was to be subsequently meted out to them, many of the prisoners taken were tortured and hanged.

A Covenanting victory was achieved at the battle of Drumclog in June of 1679, only to be followed a few short weeks later by resounding defeat at the battle of Bothwell Brig, near Hamilton, by a force commanded by the Duke of Monmouth.

Nearly 800 Covenanters were killed and 1,400 taken prisoner.

Henry Hall of Haughhead, along with other Covenanting officers who fought under the command of Robert Hamilton at the great victory at Drumclog, was also a Covenanting officer at their Bothwell Brig defeat.

Escaping the battle and seeking refuge in the

Netherlands for a number of years, he was killed
shortly after his return to Scotland after being found in
possession of what is known as the *Queensferry Paper*
– a declaration that effectively called for all-out war on
Charles II.

*Chapter three:*

# Heroes and heroines

**In later centuries and on much different bloody fields of battle, bearers of the Hall name have been rewarded with high honours and distinction.**

Born in 1885 in Kilkenny, Frederick Hall was an Irish-Canadian recipient of the Victoria Cross (VC), the highest award for valour in the face of enemy action for British and Commonwealth forces.

Immigrating to Winnipeg in 1910, he was on the field of battle only five years later on the Western Front as a company sergeant major in the 8th (Winnipeg Rifles) Battalion, Canadian Expeditionary Forces.

In April of 1915 in Belgium, during the Second Battle of Ypres, he was posthumously awarded the VC after single-handedly rescuing a number of wounded comrades before being shot dead.

In 1925, Pine Street, in Winnipeg, where he had lived, was renamed Valour Road – in honour of the astonishing fact that no less than three of Canada's VC recipients during the First World War had lived on the same block of that street; the others were Leo Clarke and Robert Shankland.

Two bearers of the Hall name were recipients during the Second World War of the Medal of Honor – the United States' highest military award for valour.

Born in 1895 in Bloom, Ohio, Lewis Hall had been a technician in Company M, 35th Infantry Regiment, 25th Infantry Division, during a Japanese attack on Mount Austen, Guadalcanal, in January 1943.

Under heavy attack and ignoring an order to withdraw, Hall and his comrade William Fournier manned a machine-gun until Hall was killed and Fournier wounded, dying from his wounds three days later.

Both men were posthumously awarded the Medal of Honor.

Born in 1921 in Stoneham, Massachusetts, George J. Hall was awarded the Medal of Honor for his bravery in action near Anzio, Italy, in May of 1944.

He had been a staff sergeant in the 135th Infantry Regiment, 34th Infantry Division, when he was severely wounded after single-handedly capturing an enemy machine-gun position.

Awarded the Medal of Honor, he died two years later as a result of the wounds he had received.

One particularly intrepid bearer of the Hall

name was the heroine Virginia Hall, recognised as having been America's greatest female spy.

Born in 1906 in Baltimore, Maryland, what was to be a highly colourful and decidedly dangerous career began as a young woman when she travelled to Europe to study – later, in 1931, being appointed a consular service clerk at the U.S. Embassy in the Polish capital of Warsaw.

Her promising diplomatic career came to an abrupt end only a year later when she had to have one of her legs amputated from the knee down and replaced with a wooden appendage after she accidentally shot herself while on a hunting trip.

She travelled to Paris shortly after the start of the Second World War in 1939, joining the Ambulance Service, and later moving to Vichy – as the unoccupied area of France was then known.

Then making her way to London after America's entry into the war, she volunteered for hazardous duty with Britain's Special Operations Executive (SOE), set up with Prime Minister Winston Churchill's remit of 'to set Europe ablaze.'

Throughout the war, after being parachuted into France, she worked for both SOE and, later, its American counterpart the Office of Strategic Services

(OSS), forerunner of the CIA, and playing a vital role in co-ordinating activities of the French Resistance movement.

Frustrating attempts by the Gestapo to run her to ground and known by several aliases that included *Mary of Lyon* and *Camille* – a frustrated Gestapo knew her as the elusive 'limping lady', and considered her 'the most dangerous of Allied spies.'

Six years after the end of the conflict, by which time she had married American OSS agent Paul Goillot, she joined the newly-formed CIA as an intelligence analyst.

The recipient of a number of honours and awards, including the Distinguished Service Cross, Virginia Hall died in 1982. She is the subject of a 2005 book by Judith L. Pearson, *The Wolves at the Door: The True Story of America's Greatest Female Spy*.

From the battlefield to the sciences, Sir James Hall, 4th Baronet of Dunglass, was the eminent Scottish geologist and geophysicist born in 1761 at Dunglass, Haddingtonshire, the son of Sir John Hall, 3rd Baronet, and Magdalen, a daughter of Sir Robert Pringle, 3rd Baronet of Stichill, Roxburghshire.

A student at Edinburgh University in the early 1780s under the renowned naturalist John Walker and the chemistry professor Joseph Black, both of whom helped to hone his scientific technique and fire his quest for further knowledge, he later travelled throughout Europe.

It was here that he scoured bookshops for the latest works on chemistry, geology and mineralogy, and also made the acquaintance of the famous French chemist Pierre Lavoisier.

Returning to Scotland, he became immersed in the study of geology, writing a number of pioneering works on the chemical composition of rock strata in addition to research on granite – while also returning to the continent to carry out in-depth studies of lava flows in Italy and the geological formations of Mount Etna and the Alps.

Also the author of a number of works on architecture and a president of the Royal Society of Edinburgh, he died in 1832.

He was the father of the naval officer and early travel writer Basil Hall, born in 1788 and who died in 1844.

Educated at the Royal High School, in his native Edinburgh, he joined the Royal Navy, being commissioned as a lieutenant in 1808 and later attaining the rank of captain.

As a naval captain, he was engaged in a number of British scientific, exploration and diplomatic missions, meticulously recording all he saw in his detailed journals – a practice in which he had been encouraged by his father.

He explored Java in 1813. Four years later he met with and interviewed Napoleon while the former French Emperor was living in lonely exile on the barren waste of the island of St Helena.

His journals served as the source for a number of books and other publications, including his grandly-titled 1823 *Extracts from a Journal written on the coasts of Chile, Peru and Mexico* and also one of the first descriptions of Korea by a European.

Author of the nine-volume *The Fragments of Voyages and Travels* and the 1829 *Travels in North America*, he also contributed to the *Encyclopaedia Britannica* and wrote scientific papers on such diverse subjects as the trade winds and comets.

*Chapter four:*

# On the world stage

**From music and acting to sport and politics, bearers of the proud name of Hall have stamped their mark at an international level.**

Beginning her stage career on Broadway at the age of 20 in the chorus line of *Shuffle Along*, **Adelaide Hall** was the American jazz singer and entertainer born in 1901 in Brooklyn, New York.

Three years after making her Broadway debut, she married a British former seaman, Bertram Hicks, who became her business manager after he opened the Big Apple nightclub in Harlem.

She began recording with Duke Ellington in 1927, producing hits that include *Creole Love* and *I Must Have That Man*, while in 1928 she was again on Broadway starring in *Blackbirds of 1928* – the most successful all-black show in Broadway's history.

She and her husband settled in Britain in 1938, and it was here that she remained until her death in 1993 – having recorded and performed with artists, in addition to Duke Ellington, who included Art Tatum, Louis Armstrong, Fats Waller and Jools Holland.

Also in the jazz genre, **Al Hall**, born in 1915 in Jacksonville, Florida and who died in 1988, was the bassist who played for artists who included Billy Hicks, Errol Garner and Benny Goodman.

In a much different musical genre, **Lynden Hall** was the singer, songwriter, arranger and record producer who won the Best Newcomer Award at the 1988 Music of Black Origins (MOBO) Awards.

Born in 1974 in Wandsworth, London, he died at the age of only 32, having released best-selling albums that include his 1997 *Medicine 4 My Pain* and the 2005 *In Between Jobs*.

Born in Edinburgh in 1936, **Robin Hall** was the Scottish folksinger who from 1960 to 1981 was a member of the popular duo Robin Hall and Jimmie MacGregor; he died in 1998.

On screen, and best known for her role from 1976 to 1988 on the long-running children's television series *Sesame Street*, **Alaina Hall** was the American actress born Bernice Ruth Reed in 1946 in Springfield, Ohio; she died in 2009.

Born in 1937 in Brighton, Alabama, **Albert Hall** is the American actor whose film credits include the 1979 *Apocalypse Now* and, from 1993, *Rookie of the Year*, while **Adrian Hall** is the English actor best known for his role as the young Jeremy Potts in the 1968 *Chitty Chitty Bang Bang*.

Born in 1959 in Staines, Middlesex, his other film credits include the 1970 *The Man Who Had Power Over Women*.

Behind the camera lens, **Conrad Hall**, born in 1926 in Papeete, Tahiti, to an American father and part-Polynesian mother, is regarded as having been one of film history's ten most influential cinematographers.

The accolade came from the International Cinematographers Guild shortly after his death in 2003.

The recipient of Academy Awards for Best Cinematography for films that include the 1969 *Butch Cassidy and the Sundance Kid* and the 2002 *Road to Perdition*, other main films in which he was involved include, from 1967, *Cool Hand Luke* and the 1973 *Electra Glide in Blue*.

He was the father of the cinematographer **Conrad Wyn Hall**, born in 1958 in Los Angeles and whose films include *Panic Room*, from 2002, and the 2005 *Two for the Money*.

Also behind the camera lens, **William Hall**, born in 1958 in Santa Barbara, California, is the writer and actor who created the two U.S. television series

*Single Guy* and *Watching Ellie* and who is also known as a news anchor on America's *Saturday Night Live* television show.

Nominated for an Academy Award for Best Director for the 1941 film *Here Comes Mr Jordan*, **Alexander Hall** was the American actor and director born in 1894 in Boston.

Engaged for a time to the actress Lucille Ball before her marriage to Desi Arnaz, he died in 1968.

A distinguished director of both theatre and film, **Sir Peter Hall** was born in 1930 in Bury St Edmonds, Suffolk.

The son of a stationmaster, he studied at Cambridge University, where he produced and acted in a number of productions, before founding the Royal Shakespeare Company in the early 1960s.

Director of the National Theatre from 1973 to 1988, he was knighted for his services to theatre in 1977, while in 1999 he was the recipient of a Laurence Olivier Award.

In the creative world of the written word, **Sarah Hall**, born in 1973 in Carlisle, Cumbria, is the English novelist and poet whose *The Electric Michelangelo* was nominated for the 2004 Man Booker Prize.

Bearers of the Hall name have also excelled in the highly competitive world of sport.

A member of the Canadian basketball team at the 1976 Olympics, **Cameron Hall** is the retired player who was born in 1957 in Hamilton, Ontario, while on the golf course **Walter Hall**, born in 1947 in Winston-Salem, is the American professional golfer whose major wins include the 2001 Canada Senior Open Championship.

Born in 1980 in Kalamazoo, Michigan, **Adam Hall** is the professional ice hockey player who, in 1999 and 2000, represented the United States at the World Junior Ice Hockey Championships.

Taking to the heavens, **Asaph Hall** was the American astronomer who, in 1877, famously discovered the moons of Mars now known as Deimos and Phobos.

Born in 1829 in Goshen, Connecticut, the son of a clockmaker, he became professor of astronomy at the U.S. Naval Observatory in Washington D.C.

In addition to discovering the moons of Mars, his many other accomplishments include determining the mass of Mars and the rotation of Saturn.

Recipient in 1879 of the Gold Medal of the Royal Astronomical Society, he died in 1907, while

Hall crater on the Moon and Asteroid 3299 Hall are named in his honour.

His son, also named Asaph, born in 1859 and who died in 1930, followed in his footsteps as an astronomer and is noted for determining the mass of Saturn.

From astronomy to politics, **Barbara Hall**, born in 1946, is the Canadian lawyer and former New Democratic Party politician who, in addition to serving as 61st Mayor of Toronto from 1994 to 1997, has also served as Chief Commissioner of the Ontario Human Rights Commission.

Also in politics, **Sir John Hall**, born in 1824 in Hull, England and who later immigrated to New Zealand, served as the Independent Party Prime Minister of New Zealand from 1879 to 1882.

Interested in women's rights, it was Hall who moved the Bill in Parliament in 1893 that gave women the right to vote – the first country in the world to do so.

Credited with having been the first person to grow a synthetic diamond under properly verifiable and witnessed procedures, Howard Tracy Hall, better known as **Tracy Hall**, was the pioneering American physical chemist born in 1919 in Ogden, Utah.

It was while working in the General Electric

Research Laboratory in Schenectady, New York, that he created a diamond through the synthesis and compression of carbon.

The recipient of a number of honours and awards, including the Chemical Pioneers Award from the American Institute of Chemists, he died in 2008.

Operating mainly in New South Wales and known as **Brave Ben Hall**, Ben Hall was the Australian bushranger born in 1837 in Wallis Plains, Hunter Valley.

Hall and his gang were reckoned to have carried out more than 100 robberies between 1863 and 1865 – although the majority of ordinary folk admired him as a Robin Hood figure.

He was finally shot and killed after being ambushed by police in 1865 and became the subject of ballads that include *The Ghost of Ben Hall*.

Another particularly colourful bearer of the Hall name was **Anthony Hall** – who claimed he was the rightful heir to the British throne.

Born in 1898 in Shropshire, he maintained he was heir through his descent from an illegitimate son of Henry VIII and the ill-fated Anne Boleyn, born before they were married.

Setting out his claim in a number of public

speeches, he also wrote a letter to King George V in 1931 – bizarrely challenging him to a duel, with the loser to be beheaded.

The monarch wisely ignored the invitation to a duel, but Hall was arrested on a number of occasions for using 'scandalous language', fined and bound over to keep the peace.

This was rather ironical, considering that Hall was actually a serving Shropshire police officer.

He died in 1947, while his story was used as the basis of John Harrison's aptly named 1999 novel *Heir Unapparent*.